The Dead Singing

FIRST EDITION, 2016

The Dead Singing
© 2016 by Michael Henson

ISBN 978-0-9972517-0-8

Except for fair use in reviews and/or scholarly considerations, no part of this book may be reproduced, performed, recorded, or otherwise transmitted without the written consent of the author and the permission of the publisher.

Cover Photo
© 2016 by Liv Kristina Henson

Author Photo by George Duchaine

MONGREL EMPIRE PRESS
NORMAN, OK

ONLINE CATALOGUE: WWW.MONGRELEMPIRE.ORG

This publisher is a proud member of

COUNCIL OF LITERARY MAGAZINES & PRESSES
www.clmp.org

Book Design by Mongrel Empire Press using iWork Pages

THE DEAD SINGING

Poems

Michael Henson

2016

Acknowledgements

The Dead Singing first appeared as a much shorter chapbook by Finishing Line Press of Georgetown, Kentucky. The poems from the Finishing Line chapbook edition have all been incorporated into this expanded edition.

The author gratefully acknowledges publication of these poems by Finishing Line Press as well as the following journals, magazines, and anthologies: *Athenaeum, Birmingham Poetry Review, Blue Collar Review, Burning River Review, Columbia Review, For a Better World: Poems and Drawings for Peace and Justice, Illinois Quarterly, Mnemosyne, Poetry Journal, Mucked, Panama Times, Pemmican, Pine Mountain Sand & Gravel, Sow's Ear Poetry Review, Still: the Journal, PoetryBay, Rock and Sling, StreetVibes, Words,* and in *Coal: an Anthology*.

Also by Michael Henson
Fiction
Ransack (West End Press)
A Small Room with Trouble on My Mind (West End Press, revised ed., Bottom Dog Press)
Tommy Perdue (MotesBooks)
The Way the World Is: the Maggie Boylan Stories (Brighthorse Books)

Poetry:
The Tao of Longing and the Body Geographic (Dos Madres Press)
Crow Call (West End Press)
The Dead Singing (chapbook edition, Finishing Line Press)
The True Story of the Resurrection and Other Poems (Wind Publications)

Contents

Introduction: The Lost Poem	1

I. Places and Seasons

Late Summer, Southern Ohio	5
Autumn	6
Winter	7
Spring	8
In the Trappist Hills	10
In the White Mountains	14
Sleepless in Portland	15
The Poets Drive East into Albuquerque	17
Coyote	18
Thanksgiving Day	19
The Beach at Nantasket	20
A Day in Winter	21
January Storm	22
Jemez, New Mexico	23
Barge on the Ohio River	24
December Rain	26
Manzanita, Oregon Coast	27
Wind Chill Factor 48 Below	28
Sycamore on the Ohio	29
Casco Viejo	31

II. I Do Not Understand What God Was Thinking

Come On Up	37
The End of the Suburbs	39
Thirty Years Ago*	40
Homage to James Wright	44
No End: for Bill Kashersky	45
Poem for Jim Trammel	46
Elegy: Patricia Clark Smith	48
3 O'clock in the Afternoon	49
Professionalism	53
Memorial for the Homeless Dead	54
Lightning at Four-Twenty-Nine	56

III. THE DAY IS COMING

They All Asked about You	61
History of the World	63
History of America	64
The Great Man	65
Shock and Awe	66
Woman of the Sidhe	67
Where Are We Going?	68
Winter Morning: D.C.	69
The Day Is Coming	70

IV. ACROSS THE PARK

Street Scene and Meditation	75
The Alleys of Over-the-Rhine	80
A Young Crow	81
On State Avenue	82
A Woman at Kroger's Explains Her Tattoo	84
The New Yorkers	85
Tommy's Off His Meds Again	87
The Light from Jimmy's Bar	88
Ohio River Nocturne	89
Across the Park	92
Note	95

Nature's a killer I won't sing to it
I hold my breath and listen to the dead singing
under the grass

—Ikkyu
from *Crow with No Mouth*
translated by Stephen Berg

Introduction: The Lost Poem

It comes on you at work.
In the middle of a meeting.
Or fishing.
Or in the rush of traffic
with a semi bearing down
and no place to pull over.
It comes on you washing dishes
and your hands are wet
and there's no paper near
and the phone just rang.
It comes on you making love
and all in your nostrils
is the smell of your lover's hair
and the odor of fresh sheets
and these stay with you
but the poem does not.
It cannot wait.
It speeds into the ozone
and we cannot know what poem it was meant to be.
It could be the poem of lost joy.
What joy?
The joy is lost with the poem.
Or the poem of tender memory.
What memory?
Lost, as all memory will be lost one day.
Or the poem of birth and death.
What birth?
And who among us is dying?
The poem would have told us,
but we could not catch it.
It could be the poem of bitterness and rage.
The poem of nails and acid.
Is it better that it should be lost?
Should we honor spite with a poem?

Could we stand
before the mirror of a poem
and see our bitter selves?
Perhaps we could,
But the poem is gone;
the mirror is empty.
So could it be the poem of blessing?
If so, then the poem is not lost.
For here, now,
I bless you with this poem.

I. Places and Seasons

Late Summer, Southern Ohio

The rains of spring are over.
The flooded pools of Big Indian,
White Oak,
Brush Creek,
Blue Creek,
and a thousand other streams
now recede, shrink, and clarify.
The banks harden
into the shape they will hold
for the rest of the season.
The stolen topsoil of the farms to the north
settles to the bottom.
The living screen of willows goes brittle.
The paper leaves rattle
at the touch of a breeze.
Sunlight spears the bluegill
among the rocks and grasses.
Smallmouth lurk beneath ledges
and in the shadow of the boulders.
They fatten on the dark minnows.

Autumn

We are startled into the season.
Acorns snap against the roof.
Walnuts thump the ground.
The paths crackle with copperhead leaves.
Everywhere, things hurry toward completion.
Pumpkins thicken in the garden
and potatoes in their dens.
The last of the apples gather sweetness.
The deer and opossum fatten desperately
against what is to come.
The purple mosques of the Canada thistles
lose heart altogether.
The green sap falls.
The lances darken.
The tendrils stiffen into frozen arabesques.
A boy with a stick
will shatter them
into a cloud
of silver splinters,
leafmeal,
spines,
dust,
seed.

Winter

Season of silence.
Snow drops through the empty halls of air.
Silence builds
sedimentary seam upon seam.
By day, by night,
the white screen falls.
Tomorrow, the slush of labor.
Tomorrow, the rasp of blades.
Tomorrow, the clatter of silicon.
For now,
the loud,
the hard
are smothered in the fall of snow.
The white mouth
swallows sound.
A shotgun
a man chopping wood
the vigilant cough of a buck
fall and die
in the bonecold air.
The truck that rattles the bridge floor
the *hish* of cars on the highway
a shout in argument
fall and die, fall and die.
All sounds rise to fall and die.

Now

listen:

sibilant lisp of the universe

Spring

First hints:
A red haze among the maples.
A great clutter of branches thrown down by a storm.
A row of daffodils that raise their baffled heads
out of the cold beds of the garden.
The light,
stretched back by the black fingers
of the trees at the horizon,
stretched back by the rooftops
at the head of the alley,
ekes out the lingering days.
The winter rains become the spring rains,
cold and persistent.
The rivers rise to their banks;
they darken with silt.
They boil coldly
in their drive to the Gulf
bearing downstream anything loose in their path.
Then, a day that ignites
green fires at the tips of the sycamores.
A day when the earth shimmers
with a dim mammalian pulse.
After the million deaths of winter,
partisan births,
clandestine cadres,
in tens and twelves,
here, and here, and in the hedges.
Everything swells.
Everything grows more numerous.
New hungers arise,
some small as the belly of a vole,
some nearly small as thought.
Others large as a field of wheat.
Still others larger than we dare name.

Everywhere the hungers assert themselves.
They stretch among the root hairs in the compost.
They call from the nests tucked in the branches of the cedars.
They quiver on the dark floor of every pond.
They weep themselves known in the houses of the poor.

In the Trappist Hills

1. Morning

Frost still lines the grasses,
still paints the stones of the path.
My shoes scuff loudly
against the frozen gravel
and a thicket
gives up its startled finches
as I pass.
Further on,
the sudden, harsh
cry of a hawk.
Six times, she cries
Eight times
Nine times
Ten!
The sun strikes gold
beneath her wings.

2. A Pond

A single cat tail
at the edge of a pond.
The pond is leaden-still,
sheeted
at the western edge
with green ice.
The sun, setting,
slants down
through the white fibers
unraveling
from the head of the cat tail.
The white parasol seeds
break loose
one by one
and float
out
over the glass of the pond,
shaken free
by a wind,
just the hint of a wind
like the breath of God
sleeping.

3. The Path into the Hills

Someone charted this path.
Someone measured the meanders
along its stations
and up into the line of hills
where I seek the highest point.
I do not know who broke the gravel
I do not know who carted the gravel
and laid the gravel
along the bed of this path.
But I am grateful
for the ones
who opened this path for me
and made a bed of crushed stone for my feet.
A path is good.
It is also good to turn off the path,
to climb the naked shoulders of the hillside
to stumble the broken shelves of limestone.
It is a harder climb.
Greenbriar, honeysuckle,
thickets of pine,
and the winterbranches bare of leaves
all pull, catch at the coat,
trip at the ankle,
and threaten the eye with whiplash.

There are things to learn from the path.
There are things to learn from the not-path.

At the peak of the knob,
I rest, I eat the small food I have brought
and I look around me.
I am alone at the hub of the world.
The wind cups my ears
and covers all other sound.
The road which brought me here

and which will take me home
is hidden by a line of trees.
Hills and ridges all around.
Pastures, fields of black furrows.
Clustered towns.
And the silent white stones of Gethsemani.

In the White Mountains

Scrambling in the bare rocks at the peak:
the chipmunks of Mount Chocorua.

Birds in black and gray:
small winged Capuchins.

Here, in the boulder's shadow:
the wind-stripped bones of a fox.
The perfect ribs still frame the thin air.
The whistle-thin legs still seem to dance.

Rain clouds form
and rush across the bare stone shoulders of the mountain.
Small mists rise
through the pines
and hemlocks.
They meet
the clouds
at the peak,
curl into the stream,
and hurry to be rain somewhere to the east.

Two ravens
find the thermals.
They growl and call.
They climb the empty ladders of air.

Sleepless in Portland

Four AM in the City of Roses:
The clang of a dumpster
wakes me for the first time.
The prostitutes of 82nd Avenue
are all sleeping by now.
The drunk woman who sang us our ABCs
is sleeping it off by now.
But the meth addict
still burns in his loneliness
The truck groans the dumpster up,
unloads it,
and sets it back down
with the same loud clang.
My companion sleeps through it all.
Smell the pines!
she said last night.
The pines,
dark sentinels
outside our door.

Six AM in the City of Roses:
The sun strikes gold
in the creosote
of the telephone pole across the street
and in the wires that swing down
to the house across the street
and in the eaves
of the house across the street
and in the throat
of the dove outside our window.

Seven AM in the City of Roses:
Time to rise at last.
How do I know?
The crow told me.
The crow!
told me!

The Poets Drive East into Albuquerque
For Fred Whitehead

Route 66 falls
straight as an Acoma arrow
into the valley of the Rio Grande.
We roll past signs of twisted neon,
the white-bearded ghosts of the Okies,
fast food endless fast food restaurants,
a pipe metal cross wreathed in plastic flowers
for some poor anonymous saint
martyred by the caesars of internal combustion.
A girl crosses Coors Road with her hands going pitapat.
A man and woman argue in the asphalt of a McDonald's.
Children burst into furious desert flower.
I want to know,
what detoured the pilgrims
who stay in these sad faux-Navaho motels?
And are they under a curse?
I want to know,
whose souls are kicking up the dust of the trailer park?
But we are silent as a pair of Trappists gone AWOL.
For the wide, scattered city lies before us.
The low, salmon-colored houses of the neighborhoods,
the sun-struck downtown towers
and above it all, solid and somnolent
as gods who have just made love,
the sun-mottled Sandia Mountains.

Coyote

The cold coyote calls
from his place in the moon-blanched meadow.
He wants to paint the pale moon
with the blood of his solitude.
So he sings his dark song
of owl whoop
and the feathers of small birds.
The night is a great black bowl
and he wants to fill it
with his lament of broken stars.
So he sets back on his haunches
and sings his sawblade song
of lost children
and the splintered cliffs of mountains.
He fills his lungs
with the oxygen of fallen cedars
and sings his song
of the paper wings of moths.
The sky is nippled with cold stars.
So he wants to sing his dark song
of cold flame
empty jars
and the sad steel of knives.

Thanksgiving Day

The river wind
pricks against the current
and small white breakers
chop against the shore.
A white gull glides low
over the gray water,
skitters to a stop,
and bobs in the shallows.
The day is silent
but for the drumming wind
and I walk this shore alone.
The air is bright, cold,
flecked with snow.
A hawk cries cold
somewhere in the trees.
My path is cumbered
with willow shoots,
driftwood, thistles,
floodborn milk jugs,
and flats of styrofoam
and, at times, I stumble.
The dark grasses tangle up my feet.
I stumble, and recover.

Sometimes, my soul rises
up from my encumberments
like a white gull in the cold.

I am lonely here, and joyous.

The Beach at Nantasket

The wind beats
against the windows
of the shuttered summer houses.
A boy whistles
against the rumpling wind.
He looks out to the cold sea,
the long, cold sea.
Seek, seek,
the cold gulls call.
They skim the white caps
of the waves.

A Day in Winter

Five cold crows
a black stave against the sun.
Mind no mind.
Wind that is no wind.
Breath that flees down the cedars of the hillside.
Nothing at all under my hat.

January Storm

A great, rattling, treebreaker wind
gusts and blusters around the house.
Windows shiver in their frames.
Nails wince in the joists.
A great, shuffling bigfoot beast of wind . . .

What is he doing out there in the dark?

Jemez, New Mexico

A dust devil stalks the plaza
peels up paperscrap
loose tobacco
and red dust gathered from the four directions
by the winds of the four directions.
The dust devil whirls
now the size of a man
now the size of a larger man
now twice the size of a man
and now disperses like a man dismembered
and settles the dust
among the dust-colored adobes of the pueblo.

Barge on the Ohio River

Under the white moon,
the white crests on the black waters.
Across the water,
the white shape of a tug
pushing before it
a line of great, rust-shouldered,
high-riding empties.
The running lights are amber and green.
A shaft of blue light
from the forecastle
touches the Kentucky shore
and the Ohio shore,
then snaps shut.
I can hear
the deep, Tibetan thrumming
of its deep-throated diesel thorax
as it passes
and I stand and watch
until it rounds the bend
and the amber light at the stern
winks out behind the Kentucky willows
and I think,
how useless is all beauty.
For I have stood here these several minutes
as the mud-colored breakers of the wake
begin to slap at the shore
and I have not moved once
to think of the condition of man
or of my insignificance in the universe.
I do not think
I will have become,
by tomorrow,
kinder or more honest.
The passing of this elegant machine
has spared no one his hunger

and no one her bruises.
I would not trade this moment
for any other,
but it has changed nothing in the suffering world.
And I do not understand,
my God,
for there you are,
strolling in the garden,
arguing Art with a bishop.

December Rain

There is something cruel in the December rain.
Sullen and metallic,
gusts pellet the face
spike the hands
and drive the homeless
into the dubious shelter
of abandoned storefronts.
The blackening leaves
congeal in the gutters
and the children
leave off shouting in the alley.
The rain sweeps the parks empty
and beats against storefront windows
with a gray, sodden warning.
Men and women stalk the streets
under the shadow of umbrellas
or, hatless,
bow their heads to the rain
as if they were taking a beating.

Behind safe windows,
we watch the driven, hammered rain
and the dark, treetop sky.
We want
anything but this
cold clockwork rain.
We want warmth.
We want light.
We want the comfort we cannot have.

Manzanita, Oregon Coast

At dawn,
mists hide the peak
of *Neah-Kah-Nie*.
Along the beach, sea litter:
great logs, stumps,
eroded planks of lumber,
and yellow stalks of kelp.
Gulls whirl in the cold wind
or scout the sands for the luckless crab.
Later, the rain drives in from the sea.
Swift, fitful, pelleting rain.
Rain in great gusts.
Fistfuls of rain.
Ragged curtains and flags of rain.
And with the rain, the clouds.
You would not know there was a mountain at all!

Wind Chill Factor 48 Below

Under the loom of the Hancock Tower
the wind rips the fur-lined people
like pages of the Tribune.
They prop each other up as they stagger and scream.

The same wind rattles the wine bottle on West Madison.
The same wind rattles the cardboard
in the windows of Uptown.
The same wind rattles the pages
of the cop's ticket book in Woodlawn.

Wind in the alley.
Wind in the kitchen.
Siren wind that fills the belly with snow.

Sycamore on the Ohio

Gaunt and precarious,
a sycamore leans out
over the winter Ohio.
In the flood season,
when the waters tear at the banks,
the black reptilian bodies of oak, cottonwood, catalpa
float downstream, half-submerged.
But this sycamore holds fast, for now,
its place in the earth.
The roots on the eroded river side reach out,
dig their mottled heels in the sand,
and brace themselves
among the beds of the mussels
and the gravelly nests where catfish spawn.
Stripped bare by the floods,
these roots are like the granite buttresses of cathedrals
or, like great vegetal pythons,
or, like the knees of gods at rest.
Behind them, the bank side roots, curtained in silt,
set out to explore the interstitial corridors of the subsoil.
They cast their nets wide in the darkness.
They pass along the stations of the mole
and follow the paths of the worm and the nematode.
They sift with their white fingers
through the mineral amalgam
of sand, leafmeal, shell, fish scale,
rusted hook, and chips of mica.
They penetrate the caskets of clay
and tell no secrets.

They press into the crevices of the layered limestone
and trace the flutes of the scalloped fossil.
They pore over shards of the Adena,
splinters of brick,
and fragments of broken glass polished like discarded jewels.
They pry among the bones of the hanged man
and touch,
as if it were a relic,
the pierced heart of someone's drowned daughter.

Casco Viejo

Panama City, 2006

1. Boys on the Plaza
In La Plaza Independencia
the barefoot boys
play futbol until dark.
Their goals:
sections of PVC pipe,
scraps of rope.
Their pitch:
the narrow space
among the bronze torsos
of the heroes.
¡Velo! they cry. ¡Velo! ¡Velo!

2. ¿Donde Esta El Internet Cafe?
The Policía del Turismo do not know.
So a woman decides she will be our guide.
She is small
and her cheeks are stark
and she is all angles and rapid gestures
and I do not know the Spanish for crackhead
but I have my suspicions
and I am not sure where she is taking us
for she speaks *muy rapidamente*
and my Spanish is small.
¿Internet Café?
Sí, sí, she says,
and we walk *muy rápidamente*
along the streets hung with laundry
where there are no women selling *molas* to the tourists.
Eventually, we will get there
and it will not look like Starbucks.
But first, she stops, suddenly.
She points:
on the wall of *la lavandería*:

a thumb-sized
thumb-colored lizard
with bright, creosote eyes.
Clo-clo, she tells us. *Clo-clo.*
Limpia su casa.

3. The Restaurant of the Tombs
We will not go
to the Restaurante Las Bóvedas
where once
the prisoners drowned
with the incoming tide.
But I stand outside
and stare for a moment
at the tables
agleam with silver
and crystal
on the white
tablecloths.

4. Shadows
Everywhere in this place, I see
shadows of Noriega,
shadows of a man of scars.

5. Restless, at Four in the Morning & Against All Advice, I Take a Walk
A man stands near our doorway.
Buenos, I say.
But he stares across the plaza
as if I am not there.
A través de la plaza
a man sorts through the trash.
On a balcony above,
in one of the squatter buildings,
a man and a woman share coffee at a cafe table.
Behind them,

the window frames are empty,
the walls are empty.
The rich abandoned this place to the poor.
Now, brick by brick,
they are buying it back.
On one corner,
silent men
load a truck
with bed frames, chairs,
cardboard boxes.
At another,
men in black uniforms
with black guns
slung from their shoulders
stand guard in the alleys
that lead to the Palace of the Herons.
I walk until I come
to the palisades above the bay.
I watch the lights of the ships
waiting in the dark.
I watch the dark waves
beat on the black rocks.

II. I Do Not Understand What God Was Thinking

Come On Up

An old man looks up
to the farmhouse on the hill.
It is late October and the sun slants
over the hilltops with an amber glint
on the weathered boards.
He would have sworn,
just two days ago,
the house stood empty.
But here it is,
with curtains in the window
a comfortable smoke in the chimney
and a half dozen dogs lazy in the yard.
And here is his old friend,
his neighbor from long ago.
Here they are at the gate at the foot of the hill
as they stood so many years ago.
They tell each other stories
they each already know,
but they tell them for the telling of them
as they used to do.
After a time,
the neighbor man says,
Come on up to the house.

The first man knows
it would be a grave discourtesy not to come.
So they will talk awhile longer.
And the neighbor man will look up to the house
and the smoke that curls from the chimney
and he will say,
I reckon she has supper on.
For the woman of the house has seen them.
Nothing special, she will say,
yet it will be the last of the pickles
and fat tomatoes just picked from the dwindling vines,

and chicken, battered and fried
until the meat is tender as butter
and green beans and mashed potatoes
and biscuits – so buttery and crisp
they must be the biscuits God eats.
And a cobbler, made sweet
with the berries the children picked
last summer, when they came from the city.
The old men will talk just a short while longer.
It is late October
and the sun sets quickly.
Soon, it will be dark.
Come on up,
one old man will say to the other.
Come on up to the house.

The End of the Suburbs

Past the last of the rectilinear houses.
Past the last lawn.
past the garden
the trumpet vines,
the roses trained on the trellis.
Onto the path
through the second-growth woods.
I know where lie the bones of the fox.
I know where the tractor rusts
behind a screen of thistles.

Thirty Years Ago*

A winter storm moves in and settles on the city streets.
The frozen gargoyles of City Hall leer from their parapets.
Frost grips the park benches with cold white fingers.
Snow dusts the eaves of the tenements
along Race Street, Vine Street, 14th
and the sad nameless alleys that run off Republic.
Snow caps the parking meters
and blinds the windows of the parked cars.
It is a deep, perfect, silencing snow
that muffles the sounds of the sirens,
the cars on Central Parkway,
the snatches of music
that thump from the jukeboxes of Main Street,
and the softened clatter of a truck being loaded.

Into the snow steps a group of ragged shadows.
Three or four at first, then more,
then tens and twelves.
They shiver, blink back the snow,
pull their second-hand coats tighter,
and stagger, step, or shuffle as they are able,
southward down Main Street.
Some talk, some grumble,
and some are silent as the snow,
but they walk in something like order, something like a march.
They walk as if, at the end of their march,
there might be something like hope.
Perhaps they are crippled by alcohol,
for they do not seem to understand
it is the job of the poor
to die silently and in some other place.
Down Main, they stumble south to 12th Street.
Those at the head of the line stop for a moment.
They puzzle, where are we supposed to go?
But someone tells them,

so they turn west and continue their march.
They do not seem to understand
it is the mission of the misguided
to lose themselves quietly,
and in some other place.
Down 12th to Walnut,
they limp and shuffle in their battered manner
and pass under the cold eye of Germania,
that great verdigris goddess, perfect in limb and posture.
But they ignore her; they do not look up.
They do not seem to understand
it is the job of the broken to keep on breaking,
quietly, and in some other place.
Past Walnut, they cross Jackson where a prostitute eyes them.
She seems to see herself in them
and she stamps her foot for warmth and turns away.

The women among the shadows mutter something
and the men look down
and they all keep marching.
They do not seem to understand
it is the task of the scorned
to bury their pain down the road
in some quiet, distant place.
The shadows cross into the glare of Vine Street
and the light is not kind
for it glitters on their snowy rags
and lights the broken places on their cheeks
and marks the red rims that circle their eyes.
But they march on. They do not seem to understand
it is the duty of the damaged
to hide their broken bodies
quietly and in some distant place.
They march their shivering march past Glossinger's
and as they march, some gaze like lovers
into the darkened windows
for they have already begun to ache and shiver

for the wine that waits there.
But they march and tremble
and they do not seem to understand
it is the responsibility of the fallen
to whisper their sins to a cold, clay confessional
in some distant place.
They march past Race Street
and the park with its great black trees
and some look sidelong to watch the park fill up with snow.

They keep on, one after another,
for they do not seem to understand
it is in the interest of all
that the abandoned take their loss
to a quiet empty field in some distant place.
Down they march to Elm
where they glance toward the floodlights facing Music Hall
and they do not seem to understand
it is the obligation of the undertaught
to spare the senses of the cultured
and to die, quietly. In some other place, Not here.
But the ragged shadows march on,
just a few more stumbling steps
and through these doors against all law,
all rule, all duty for the poor
that they might find warmth,
and a little food
and a chance at life.
Through these doors,
these lawless doors.
Right here,
and not in some distant place.

Thirty years have passed.
I cannot tell you
if these shadows lived or dutifully died.
But I know the doggish cold

still follows at the heels of the poor.
The hawkish wind still whistles down the alleys.
The gargoyles of City hall
test their wings and wait their orders.
But the arrogant poor still march.
They walk their ragged, crooked mile
ignorant of law or duty
in search of a little warmth, a little food,
a little more of life than others would allow them.

We have marched through the snows and suns of thirty years.
Many have come and gone through these doors.
And we honor each of them.
For here, in this place,
we renounce the law that says the poor must die
for the comfort of the comfortable.
We abrogate the rule that says
a woman must freeze
for the warmth of the well-housed
or that a child must starve
to feed the well-fed.
Here today, we declare,
there is no law but the law of love.
There is no rule but the rule of justice.
There is no duty but the duty of hope.

Homage to James Wright

Mists climb the valley walls—
ghosts of the whores of Wheeling.
They twine among the stacks of the rusting mills
like the tendrils of a vine.
From the bridge,
the river is smooth as green glass.
Below, the long knives of the gar
track the schools of shad.
The slender shadows of the caddis
shed their clay cases, rise,
and join the larger shadows
of the darkling swallows.
In the mucky bottoms,
drowned men stir.
They startle the drowsing catfish.
Their wives,
their white-breasted wives
wait for them
in the star-clustered branches
of the sycamores.

No End: for Bill Kashersky

This silent carpenter
laid down his hammer at the last,
the final nail made fast.

The whisper of his saw
is mute; his level and his square
can measure no more care.

No yardstick now, no way
to read the blueprint of his pain.
Only shavings from a plane,

some chipped and sanded memories,
the blue dust from his chalk to chart
the true line of his heart.

In the sawdust and shavings
of a lumbered life cut short we sift
for something of a gift.

We know the plumb-line truth
is that he loved—the house he framed
will stand. His wounded name

will live in love, for of
such gifting carpentry, my friend,
there is no end, there is
no end.

Poem for Jim Trammel

On the banks of the Kanawha River
with the banks of Charleston at my back,
I watched the dark swallows
wheel over the water
until they were shadows,
until they were nothing.
A mile downstream
a barge's lean blue light
cut the watercrests.
So I crossed the bridge.

I found you under the steps,
wondering with me:
When the hell will this place open up?

Because,
in Charleston, West Virginia
the station doesn't open up til midnight
and the Cincinnati train doesn't leave til three.

They'd taken out all the benches
so we sat on the quarrystone stoop
and traded stories
while the highway shuddered over us:
    Your father marched with Mother Jones.
    The night before Blair Mountain
    she slept in your house.
    You were one year old.

For four hours we drank good whiskey in the cold.
And every hour the trains exploded past us:
    coal car coal car coal car coal car
They obliterated the mandolin.
They obliterated your stories.
They even covered up your cough.

You don't have Black Lung, Jim Trammel.
The doctor said so.
You coughed until the plastic
they put in for your stomach buckled
and you spit good whiskey out onto the stone.
But you don't have Black Lung.

You were going to Chicago,
so they made us take separate cars.
But all that rattling night long,
past the night shifts and the sleeping farms,
your red cough shook the rails.

Elegy: Patricia Clark Smith

Once more into the desert, my friend.
Once more, up into the Acoma air.
What do you see, now,
that you could not see before?
What stories do they tell there,
in the land of the lost lake?
Tell me quickly, before you go.
Before I lose you in the light
that strikes like a diamond
from the rose of the Sandia.
Quickly! Quickly,
Your voice is so small.

3 O'clock in the Afternoon
a poem for John Crawford

Three o'clock:
the hour sweeps westward across the continent
and, at the print shop, it is change of shift.
The ink man waits near the clock.
His hands are stained red.
His face is stained red.
The card in his hand is smudged with red.
He is colored with the marks of his labor.
At the mine,
the man-trip skids to a halt
and the blackening miners step to the bathhouse.
At McDonald's
a girl dreams at the drive-thru window.
She never looks at the eyes of the customers.
She barely looks at the keys of her computer.
In the prison laundry
a trusty stacks the last load of the day.
The guard yawns.
The UPS man has fallen behind.
Ten more deliveries
and will he ever get them done on time?
The prostitute swings her legs out of a man's car,
her seventh this day and she is tired
and she aches from stalking the sidewalk
and she aches from all the smiling
and all she wants is to go home.
The carpenter
will get overtime tonight
among the clatter of lumber.
A secretary stares into the monitor.
Her wrists ache from the carpal tunnel
but there is just this last report to get out.
A teacher
gathers his students' papers into a folder.

How will he get them all graded by morning?
The Wal-Mart greeter
sees an old friend from the plant.
Still working? The old friend asks.
Oh yeah, he says. Oh yeah.
At the airport,
the clerk punches up another boarding pass.
A farmer, standing in a sea of wheat,
silently curses his broke-down combine.
The hour continues across the time zones.
It crosses rivers, mountains, suburban malls
and finds a kid in an Iowa grocery store
He lines the cans of vegetables
and gazes down the aisle toward the cashier,
the one he wishes would talk to him,
as she searches a bag of rice for its bar code.
An insurance adjuster in a Texas junkyard
ponders the hulk of a crumpled SUV.
She will total it
and she will ponder,
how did that boy ever get out alive?
In El Paso
a clerk sells the small cigars
to the boys who sell crack on the corner,
At home, in Lebanon,
he never saw such things.
And in Albuquerque,
the day manager of the Route 66 Hostel
steps outside for a cigarette.
There is a man up the street,
raging at the air,
and she worries a little
for yesterday,
he tried to grab her by the wrist.
She has handled worse,
but still...
And somewhere in the wheat of the central time zone,

a bookseller shuts the trunk of his car.
The miles are high.
The tires are thin.
But he checks his maps
and calculates the hours to his next stop.
In the onion field
a woman lays down her short-handled hoe.
She jumps onto the back of the truck with the others.
A mechanic pulls the torque wrench.
A waitress serves up rice and beans.
A gardener throws down another bag of mulch.
A tailor chalks the leg of a suit.
This is the sad ballet of labor.
This is the moving body of a nation.
This is your America, my friend,
my dear John,
you, of the Whitman smile,
you, of the Wobbly dream,
you, with your hand on the wheel of story,
son of the angels of the prairie,
beloved bookmule
socialist Bodhisattva.
The hour moves westward and dies in the Pacific
and a new hour rises.
The new century nestles in the cradle of the old
as each hour is cradled in the last.
And unless we know how each hour passes
one into the next as
fall, winter, spring, summer
first shift, second shift, third
we go blind and defenseless
into a soul-breaking world.
And so the bookseller,
memorykeeper
bibliopilgrim
guardian of the divergent word
secret hero of this poem

and embodiment of all who people it,
pulls the gearshift out of park,
muscles the car onto the Interstate
and proceeds to follow the golden hour westward
hour after hour after hour

Professionalism

I
"If you leave people
to develop their own
resources
for part of the time,
they respond better
to therapy.
It stiffens them."

II
It's what the winos call the hawk:
the winter wind that strikes like a hunter.
The center was closed.
His feet were freezing.
So he developed his own resource.
The boards were already pulled off
the back door of his resource,
so he had no trouble getting in.

III
Close your textbooks.
He stiffened.
But he didn't respond.

Memorial for the Homeless Dead
December '07

The winter wind they call the Hawk
rounds the corner of the season
and skitters the last leaves to the fencelines.
We stand in a park with a paper in our hands
and down the paper runs a list of names.
None of the names will answer if we call them
but we read them to remember that they had names,
these people of the underbridge,
the condominiums of the shelters,
the apartments of park benches,
the cardboard havens and bedrooms of the poor.
What can we know about these names but that they died
—some in the usual way.
and some in ways it hurts to think on.
They died of violence, accident, and neglect.
They died of untreated disease,
of over-dose and under-attention.
They were cold, they were hungry,
they were sick, and they died.
And now they are nothing but a list of names
running off into the wind.
The Hawk sweeps the corner of the shivering season
and the cold grass is stiff around our shoes.
We stand in a park with our pockets full of wind
and nothing in our hands but these pages full of names
and the names are fading from our sight.
They were cold, they were hungry, they were sick.
They were over-dosed and under-funded,
displaced from the neighborhood of the living
and now their names trickle into the cold, stiff grass.
The Hawk tests the currents of the turning season
and strips the warmth from the downtown towers.
We stand in a park with our hats full of dust and we ask,
who decided which doors would open and

who decided which doors would close
and who decided these names
would be on the list that we read this day?
They were cold, they were tired,
they were gentrified and they died
and now their names fade into the light.
The Hawk calls once in the sweep of the changing season
and wickers away the last of the leaves.
We stand in a park with our hands full of light
and in the light a list of eternal names.
They were cold, they were sick, they were hungry.
They were over-dosed and under-guided and they died.
If we call these names now and it seems they do not answer,
we can learn to listen in the grass, in the wind,
in the shower of sunlight that falls around us.
We can listen in the cold cry of the Hawk.
Listen close:
They are a whisper now on the tongue of God.
We call their names to remember they had names,
these people of the underbridge,
the condominiums of the shelters,
the apartments of park benches,
the cardboard havens and bedrooms of the poor.

Lightning at Four-Twenty-Nine
a poem for Aralee Strange

It is four in the morning on Main Street
and a hint of rain lurks in the west.
The poet leans out her window and waits.
The lights of the street lamps show
only a nighthawk snatching at the moths that circle the lamps
and the black crisscross of the fire escapes
on the buildings across the street
and the black web of her own.
It is four-o-three in the morning
and the hint of rain moves in with a low rumble.
She raises the window to step onto the fire escape
and the metal of it rings under her feet.
She looks upstreet and down
and all is quiet on Main.
At four-o-five in the morning
somewhere, a garbage truck raises a dumpster
and groans the garbage down its maw.
Somewhere, a siren wails.
Somewhere, a dog barks.
Somewhere, someone curses the dog.
But on Main Street, all is quiet but for her own breath
and the distant rumble of the incoming rain.
At four twelve in the morning,
the hint of rain grows stronger; a wind picks up.
It skips a can down the sidewalk and sails a scrap of paper
nearly to the level of her eye
and brings it down to a Main Street landing.
At four-fourteen, a cat,
made nervous by the wind,
leaves its hidden place
for another hidden place.
The nighthawk gathers the last of its moths
and goes to nest.
At four-eighteen in the morning,

thunder rumbles in the distance
and lightning crackles the distant sky.
A man emerges from a doorway
with a bundle on his back
and turns down the alley in search of better shelter.
At four-twenty-one in the morning,
the thunder rumbles closer and
the lightning encandles the downtown towers
but the poet does not move.
She stays in her watching place
until she feels the first, hinted droplets on her hands.

At four-twenty-one in the morning
she feels the earthbreak rumble;
she feels the crack of lightning strike her cheek
and Main Street, illuminated, unfolds in the flash.
There stand the women and men of her story.
In the space of an instant
they stand in place like actors on a stage.
She has given them no names.
They offer her not yet a word or gesture.
But they stand, and are gone, light-limned,
in a clarity she cannot yet shape with words.
At four-twenty-seven in the morning,
the rain, grown fat and persistent,
drives her back through her window and into her room.
The lightning has marked her cheek
and left her body humming with what she has seen.
At four twenty-nine in the morning,
all is silent but for the rain.
She turns to her desk,
picks up a pencil,
and takes her lightning to the page.

Poem for Esme

I do not understand what God was thinking
when the earth split and swallowed the song.
A stippled hawk barked across the sky.
The caterpillar dog howled in the pit of the forest.
And in the forest, the silent, littered forest
chapeled itself a chapel out the tangled limb and vine
and fractured flowers of the grass.

There is a circle broken now.
There is a cello strangled and its heart torn open.
There is an aria choking in the throat of the guitar.
The world is a tangled, tumble-down fracturing place.
And we have only a little riddle of a song
to make it holy.
And still the earth cracked open and swallowed the song.
So I do not understand what God was thinking.

Can you open the gates of the sea?
Can you mine the sky?
Can your arms embrace the shivering earth?
We are small, you see, too small
to ever understand what God was thinking.

But I will make my little fiddling song,
my twelve bars with the bark of the hawk,
my little fractured chapel of a song.
I will dance my little stumbling dance of a poem
up through the halls of the hawk
and to the workshop of the weather.
For there is no place to take my complaint
but to God.

Though I do not understand what God was thinking.

III. The Day Is Coming

They All Asked about You

I went down to the city of light,
and they all asked about you.
The preachers, the sellers,
the man with pale flowers,
the cops gliding by in their big white cruisers,
they all asked.
The prostitute sighing her continuous sigh,
the girl with one eye bruised,
the children of the cobbled alley,
the postman with the heavy news,
they all asked.
They all asked about you.

I went down to the city of the sea,
and they all asked about you.
The mussels and starfish,
the sharks and the barnacles
and the otters in their castles of kelp,
they all asked.
The fishermen winching at their sodden nets,
the women stitching at the shore,
the cold gulls above them, screening the sands,
and the briny things clustered in the scuds of foam,
they all asked.
They all asked about you.

I went down to the city of oblivion,
and they all asked about you.
Someone mumbled through an opiate haze.
Someone muttered through an alcoholic mist.
They all asked.
The boy lowered his bag of glue
and the crackhead his pipe of dream.
The needle-freak set down his shivering spike
and a girl let the smoke drift from her mouth.

Each addled neuron knew your name.
They all asked.
They all asked about you.

I went down to the city of poets,
and they all asked about you.
In iambics and sestinas
and in yawping free verse,
they all rhythmically asked.
There was one who risked all for seven broken lines,
and there was one who stood coughing in an empty tower,
and there was one who built pyramids of abstract syllables,
and there was one whose voice was a broken trumpet.
All of these and a chorus of lyrical Greeks,
they all asked.
They all asked about you.

Then I went down to the city of earth,
and they all asked about you.
The ants and the centipedes,
the pill bugs and slugs
chewed out the words with their loamy mouths.
Mute as the mole in their vegetal manner,
they all asked.
And even the dead, in their earthen cathedrals,
lit their dark candles
and chanted for you their continuous psalm.
They all asked.
They all asked about you.

History of the World

Sacrifice and betrayal:
it's the whole story.
Red flags go out
Palm branches are thrown down.
Hope lifts
The heart swells
Brother looks at brother
Sister looks at sister
with a clear, unfettered eye.
Out of the mangers of the earth
spill wheat and martyrs.

Then the legionnaires step up.
Tanks roll.
Dollars go on the march.
The great red eye of television
fills up with victims.

History of America

First,
the little starving settlements
on the edge of the continent.
The rest of the continent waiting to be taken.
Then, the settled towns.
Then, the urgent, muscular cities.
And now,
these spreading,
brain-shaped metropoli
stitched together with asphalt and silicon.
Always pushing to the edges,
always the taking of the land—
from one, then another.
There was war,
then there was not-war.
There were slaves,
then there were not-slaves.
Someone wins,
someone loses
some resist
same fail
Some take the money
and fall into the deep moral sleep
that makes all this dreaming possible.

The Great Man

The vigilance of a great man
is the tooth of a fox
at the neck of a vole.
The breath of a great man
blesses all his projects
and withers the hopes of his enemies.
The will of a great man
rains on his people.
Day and night,
day and night
it drenches all otherwill.
The voice of a great man
rings like a metal dollar
on a marble counter.
The potency of a great man
has no purpose
but to bear all before it
like a flood
or a powerful wind.
The mind of a great man
is not bothered by contradiction,
is not worried with truth or lie,
is not disturbed by the thoughts of others.
The stride of a great man
is certain
and is not broken
by the bodies in his path.

Shock and Awe

Only men who have made their souls small
can contemplate such things.
Only men with minds abstracted
can murder with untroubled hearts.
These men have made their souls small
but their minds are very large.
The pages of their books
ripple with muscular theory.
The screens of their computers
thrill with graphics.
Their powerful search engines
discover and delete
every micron of resistance.
They have charted destruction
down to the megabyte.
The color of sand,
the taste of salt,
the prickle of heat,
the weight of a piece of fruit
are nothing to these men.
For their souls are small,
made smaller with every lie,
and their minds are abstracted
and augmented,
fed daily on megahertz and silicon.
Swollen with dollars and pride,
the inflated minds stride down the broken avenues.
These men would be like gods
were their souls not so small.

Woman of the Sidhe

She,
of the straight back.
She,
of the white cone breasts.
At her shoulder,
a green cloak
clasped
by a red-gold brooch.
At her side,
a sword with a hilt of horn.
Her long feet grip the turf.
Her long jaw tightens.
Beyond are the fields of red cloaked warriors.
Three hawks whirl in the sky above her.
She has a crown of hawks!
With a hard green eye
she watches at the ford.
Blood washes down with the waters.

Where Are We Going?

I do not know,
but there are children on the road.
Some bear weapons,
sleek in the barrel,
solid in the stock.
Some bear books.
Some bear empty bowls.
As they march,
they grow
and some grow tall
and they have the strength
of the willows that lean over the river
and some grow frail
as the cattails that line the ditch.
We plod along
with our housey burdens
and the children run ahead
and some run into the long distance
remote and indiscernible as dust.
Others run for a span.
They drop to the side of the road.
They watch us from the willows
with their solemn saucery eyes.
They want to know,
Where are we going?

Winter Morning: D.C.

1. Grey-wing gulls fly over the parkway.
    They do not see the traffic,
    nor beyond,
    the crowding of the tenements.
    They are looking for the sea,
    for a white crest,
    a silver fin.

    Lawyers fly in
    on wings that sweat with gasoline.
    They are looking for a settlement.
    No one knows what they do not see.

2. This is a city of weight:
    Concrete
            stone
                    emblems of brass
    The rains of the night
    gray the sides of the monuments.

3. Here is the congress of cold.
    I am afraid of the rattle in the leaves.
    I fear the hum in every switchbox
    and the smell of ink in the daily news.

4. In the offices,
    at Treasury, at Justice,
    computers warm.
    Printers start
    a beaucratic clatter.

    At the Pentagon,
    small brown children
    drown in the morning coffee.

The Day Is Coming

The day is coming.
Put on your boots.
The blastula earth swells.
It crackles with nerve.
Lights flicker through the east.
Strange molecules rattle in the air like gravel.
The goat sniffs once
and trots to the edge of the meadow.
Some new thing is birthing.
The day is coming.
What are you doing?
Put on your nativity.

The day is coming.
Put on your coat.
A boy walks into the desert
with his death in his arms.
Smoke drifts across the valley floor.
A woman flings dust by the handful into the barren air.
The raven watches from his post.
He calls, three times, five times, seven.
Some new thing suffers.
The day is coming.
What are you dreaming?
Put on your poverty.

The day is coming.
Put on your hat.
A broken man walks toward the distant mountains.
Monks chant away the dark hours.
A woman builds a song, stone by stone.
Even the mole has found a voice.

(Put your ear to the mouth of his tunnel;
hear him grumble.)
Some new story tells itself.
The day is coming.
What are you speaking?
Put on your wisdom.

The day is coming.
Pick up your pack.
The spears of night rattle in the alley.
In the woods, a sound of grinding steel.
In the street, a sound of dying leaves.
A man takes his place against a wall.
A woman takes her place
in a field of refugees.
Some new cross takes its nails.
The day is coming.
What are you dying?
Put on your resurrection.

IV. ACROSS THE PARK

Street Scene and Meditation

A bright, bittercold day:
A woman and four children
gather to cross
at Fourteenth and Vine.
The woman is white, the children are black,
and it seems this woman is an interloper here.
For she looks like someone's grandmother
but she does not look like theirs.
And the oldest girl
—she may be twelve—
is clearly in command.
She has the smaller ones linked,
hand to hand,
lined up at the curb like marchers
and they are packed,
identically,
in bright, insulated coats,
hooded, bundled, and immobilized
like fine china packed for shipping.
They are bright-colored beauties
admirably prepared and protected
for the cold bitter air of Vine Street.
But the woman is bare-handed,
dressed shabby and out of season
in a camel-colored cloth coat
with a kerchief knotted at her chin.
She looks like women I have seen
in coal camps
or country stores
or outside storefront churches
on Wednesday nights after services.
These are women
of great density,
made solid
by grief and wisdom.

But this old woman
has gone out of focus;
she weaves a little
as she leans toward the youngest
the wide-eyed one,
and extends a tipsy hand
to take him by the mitten.
For a moment, she wobbles,
and it seems she might mislead
this wide-eyed one
into the teeth of the traffic.
The girl, from her end of the line,
watches with a dubious eye.

What happened next?
I cannot tell you.
I only saw them for a moment,
but I remember,
photographically,
the proud, wary eye of the girl,
the wobbling way the woman leaned forward,
and the four marks,
four parallel marks,
driving downward
like an inverted stave of music,
scratched into the flesh of the woman's cheek.

I cannot think
who would make such marks
on such a woman.

From one winter into another,
I have carried this image:
Three young children in a line,
the competent, suspicious girl,
the marked, unsteady woman,
and around them,

the traffic on Vine in motion,
the traffic on Fourteenth at rest,
the vigilant and reposed dope boys leaning
against the boarded windows of the pool hall,
and around them all
that maze of brick and neon,
signboards, walk lights, glass,
vinyl, plywood, chrome,
paper, asphalt, plastic, and,
in the path of a passing truck,
a plume of diesel smoke
descending.
What more do I know of them?
Nothing more than what I have told.
I had a task before me at the time.
I jaywalked past them
to the hardware for a pound of nails
and I did not look back.
I stood in line to pay my money
and did not think,
until too late,
I had witnessed
a moment of afflicted grace.

For this girl,
of the defiant, almost-adolescent eye,
had a task:
to weave these children
from one place to another,
through the color and danger of the street.
And was that damaged woman
one of their dangers?
The girl seemed to think so,
and she knows her world much better than I.
She knows her world
far better than a child should know it.

But this toddling,
someone's-grandmother-looking woman
with her strange parallel marks
has, I think, a sad, unknowable story.
It seems her grandmother brain
has been unmoored
by wine
or maybe OxyContin.
Her addled angels
have failed to guard her
and she has been marked and shamed
in ways I cannot know.
Perhaps she hoped,
in that bright and penitential day
to bring herself a moment
of resurrected wholeness.
Perhaps she was trying
awkwardly to do right,
a saintly inebriate,
blind guide,
unprotected protector,
a broken Bodhissatva,
a being
holy and deluded
in a place
where even blessedness is fractured.
We are here to do such kindness as we can,
however we may stumble.
We are here to guide each other
through perilous crossings.
But we live in a confusion
of conflicted blessings.
We are wise to be wary of each other.

This child-mother
and the grandmother-looking woman
snapped in and out of my life

in a moment.
I never saw them again.
I do not know what crossings they now face.
But I have a prayer for them,
and for myself:

Forgive us our sanctified errors.
Help us know the marks of our failure.
Grant us a wary eye.
Let us stumble into compassion.

The Alleys of Over-the-Rhine

These are the hidden back-door by-ways,
dark and seemingly nameless as the paths of forests.

Cool and dark in the blaze of summer.
Cold and dark in the man-killing winter.

Locus of the mysteries of death and conception.
Retreat of the homeless and the hunted.

Paved with brick and curbed with stone,
littered with broken glass,
wasted syringes,
and wilted condoms...

Nothing grows here but the moss on the walls,
nothing but the grass in the seams of brick and stone.

At night, lit but the distant moons of the streetlamps,
the homeless find a cold and stony sleep.

No one sings here but the lonely inebriate, no lifts a prayer,
Only the desperate priest of the needle,
only the acolyte of the pipe.

A Young Crow

A young crow alights at the side of the road:
He has found a roadkill possum
in the gravel at the berm.
In his delight,
he clucks,
little rooky clucks,
and he struts around his find.
The opaline eyes draw his attention
for they are soft and glossy.
He pikes them out
and enjoys them
and his appetite is charged.
But first,
a car glides down the gravel toward him
and he flaps to the fenceline to wait.
The car passes
the dust settles
and the young crow returns
to his interrupted project.
He hammers around the head
the shoulders
and finds
only the flavorless hairs.
But his nostrils are keen
and they tell him,
Pluck, pluck,
and he plucks until
he strips out
a bare place
and he mines the warm flesh
and delights, delights!
in the savory thing
he has uncovered.

This is how the poet works.

On State Avenue

At the corner,
near the Mexican store,
I see a poor, staggering prostitute.
(I do not call her that
but that is what people call her.)
She has just stumbled
out of some man's car
and her body is bent
leftward
in a stumbling, distorted manner
like a bow or an arc
bent perhaps
by the moons of heroin
or by the prodding of crack cocaine
or by the distortions of her labor
serving men
in the cramped front seats of cars.
She has a name,
tattooed at her neck
like a shackle
and her teeth
are gone clouded and gray
and there is to her something
so twisted and damaged
and childlike and holy and pitiable
that I cannot understand
how any man would want to have her.
But the men do have her.
Again and again
I see them leave her on the street
near the Mexican store
in her little shackled body
bent and staggering
as if one side drives her
perpetually forward

and the other drags back
like a child
tugged down the street
by an impatient hand.

A Woman at Kroger's Explains Her Tattoo

Long story short—
her grandbaby didn't live.
A net of veins gone wild
rare disease
operations
procedures
runs to the hospital
internal bleeding.
Four years old
and he drowned in his own blood.
She turns her leg to show me:
his perfect image
inked into her calf.

The New Yorkers

I wander the vast grieving circuits of the city of New York
and bump against so much density of life.
At every corner, down every avenue
so much undiscovered human complexity
in the intricate sadness of Brooklyn and Queens
and the Bronx and Staten Island and
the smoldering promontories of Manhattan.
For each window washer
shoulders the cross of his own story.
Each woman with a baby on her hip.
is propelled by her own daemonic energy.
So many polishers of nails.
So many sellers of knishes and sushi.
So many gridlocked cabbies and truckers.
So many doormen pierced by the fierce New York winds.
So many lawyers and nurses and students
speaking so many languages
snatched from every corner and cattle track of the globe.
And all in a rush!
All of them step out with long straight legs;
all of them look forward in their intent New York manner
and all of them stride stride stride
to the bus, to the cab
to the belly of the subway station.
They whirl through the gates
and clatter all-at-once down the stairs
and know exactly which way to turn
until they reach the dark platform.
There, they wait,
motionless and potent as batteries.
Each man, each woman, each child
pulses with an electric, third-rail energy.
They poise at the edge;
they gaze toward the dark,
they tense like runners at the block

they listen for the tympanic thunder
of iron wheel on iron rail
until the train explodes out of the tunnel
with a clatter and blur and roar of metallic danger.
It threatens them no more
than the house cat that glides past the couch,
And yet it is this tigerish,
springing and metallic,
thundering thing.
And they do not retreat; they step even closer
as if they want to embrace the car.
But no, they pause, pause,
and with a sudden halt to the clatter and rush
the car stops.
The gates open,
an electronic voice chants the name of the station,
and the people of the platform pause again
and gather energy to step on as the others step off.
And I see that all this strict and relentless movement
is a vast and solemn dance.
Though I cannot hear the music
and I stumble in my bumpkin manner
along the streets and up and down the stairs of the subway,
all around me the New Yorkers
continue their kinespheric arc and swerve.
their complicated choreography of iron and electricity.
Astonished,
I gaze at the tall spires of the buildings
and the corner bodegas
and the hustlers of Times Square
and the huddling homeless
and the grim police
and the saddened men at the fire station
and I wonder at the steps
and I wonder at the turns
of this dance
of the ballistic and elegiac New Yorkers.

Tommy's Off His Meds Again

Tommy's gone off his meds again.
Tommy's become the angriest of men.
He curses all day and all night when
He flips and goes off his meds again.

The day is long and the night is short.
He bristles at everything; his body is a fort.
When he speaks his word is a rifle's report.
The night is long and the day is short.

The children mock him, the children jeer.
The smoke at his eye, the red at his ear.
They cannot bless what they're taught to fear.
So all night they mock and all day they jeer.

But he's in his own world and his world's locked up tight.
He guards it by day and watches by night.
He's wary of all that falls in his sight.
His world is a fortress, he has it locked tight.

For Tommy's gone off his meds again.
He curses all day and all night and then
He curses the dawn and starts over at ten
Now he's flipped and gone off his meds again.

The Light from Jimmy's Bar
Beckley, West Virginia
For P.J. Laska

Midnight, Saturday,
I step to the cabin porch
and piss over the rail
like an old mad monk.
Up the hill, high above me,
the great, blue-tinted
moon-shaped lamp
that guards the lot at Jimmy's Bar.
Rap music thumps in the distance
and cars rumble
along Kanawha Boulevard,
but Sarge closed up hours ago
and the parking lot of Jimmy's Bar
is silent and deserted.
There is no moonlight,
but the lamp from Jimmy's Bar will do,
for the blue light falls through the trees
and is split
by the oak leaves
into pale lances
that spear
the leaves of the rhododendron
and silver the eaves of the cabin
and shroud the raised arms of the dogwood.
Mists rise from the dark corners of the yard
like the ghosts of the miners of Sand Creek.
Their lamps search
among the composting fiddleheads.

I stand in the dark and stare
like an old mad monk.
It might as well be the moon,
so lovely is the light from Jimmy's Bar.

Ohio River Nocturne

Late summer: an evening walk
on the banks of the shining, remorseful river:
There has been no rain for weeks
to erode the upriver farms,
and the water is a clear, oceanic green.
A cloud of minnows
maneuvering to evade a marauding bass
darkens the green.
A pleasure boat
the size of an Irish cottage
putters near the Kentucky shore.
Up at the bend,
a string of barges bears downstream
a broken mountain of West Virginia coal.
The waterline is down;
we walk along a bed of sand
studded with gravel, mussel shells,
shards of glass polished smooth as opal,
and, left by fishermen,
cans of corn
cardboard beer cases and
malodorous tubs of chicken liver.

And here, among the cakes of silt,
and shards of styrofoam
driftwood
steel drums half-buried
is the eyeless corpse of a washed-up catfish.

And here is a social security card of someone—
Let's not name her—
drifted down from someplace upstream.
Muddied and a little scratched and creased,
it has survived because
the I-won't-name-her woman from Someplace Upstream

thought to have it sheathed in plastic.

And this card is not the only plastic here,
for we see, littered by the careless floods of spring,
plastic balls in red and green,
plastic bottles of every shape and shade,
plastic bumpers from wrecked Toyotas,
little, tragic-looking, lost, drowned plastic dolls,
plastic weapon toys,
plastic everything because it floats so well
and is the emblematic product of our society.
And it is all very sad.

And yet I am glad to be here
and if I squint a little
and think a little backwards
she is still a beautiful river, the ancient motherwater
her surface bright and unspoiled
her banks lined with sycamore and willow
as she was before she was burdened with dams
before the invasions of benzene and fecal coliform
before she was crossed with the barges of broken coal.
So we are only a little sad and we turn to go home.

Up in the woods, a low lonely warble.
Three men,
arranged along a fallen tree they have taken for a bench,
listen: A fourth sings a tragic ballad.
The voice of the singer is harsh as that of a heron
and he is drunk as the rest of them
and I cannot make out the words
nor can I follow the melody
but I know it is a tragic ballad
for he is high and he is lonesome
and this is the river of tragic ballads.
Perhaps it is a cirrhotic version of "Banks of the Ohio."
It is impossible to tell.

But the other men listen patiently to their friend
and they nod in time to the song.
I know these men
and I know they are broken
by labor, grief, and alcohol
and I know they are continuing to break
even at this moment,
for it is clear from the spidering red in their faces
and the sag in their shoulders
and the patience they give
to this heron-croak ballad.
I greet them briefly,
so as to honor the song
and to honor the shreds they retain of broken dignity.
One salutes me with his can of beer
and I would stay and listen
and be their companion
but I cannot bear to watch them
dying by the cluttered and darkening banks
of the barge-bearing,
silt-shouldered,
fish-rich
ballad-tragic river.

Across the Park

Across the park
I see a woman
and she is dancing down the sidewalk.
There is too much of her
and everything movable is moving
but she is graceful
and her step is slow and smooth.
A set of headphones
nestles in her braids
and I do not know what she hears
among the evening traffic
of West Eighth Street.
She steps and stops
rocks forward at the neck
pecks at the air with her hand.
She steps and stops
rocks forward at the neck
pecks at the air with her hand
steps
stops
rocks
pecks
to the music
that is wrapped around her head
until
she sees that I am staring
and she
stops.

I am in awe of her
but she does not know that
so she
stops her dance
and slowly walks her sidewalk
until she thinks
I may not hear.

And then she sings.

Note

Thirty Years Ago
Written on the occasion of the thirtieth anniversary of the midnight move of Cincinnati's Drop Inn Center shelterhouse from dilapidated quarters on Main Street to a site on 12th Street. At the behest of City Council and local developers, the City of Cincinnati's Health Department had condemned the Main Street site. Hoping to shut down homeless services altogether, the Health Department had also withheld approval of any alternate site. However, advocates for the homeless had secretly negotiated purchase of the old headquarters of Teamsters Local 100. They rented a couple of U-Haul trucks and at midnight on Friday night January 13, 1978, during a blinding snowstorm, they moved the entire facility—mats, kitchen, office furniture, and all. By Monday morning, when city offices opened, the center had been housing the homeless all weekend and continued to do so for decades after.

Michael Henson is author of four collections of poetry and four books of fiction, including *The Way the World Is: the Maggie Boylan Stories*, which won the 2014 Brighthorse Prize in Short Fiction. He is co-editor of *Pine Mountain Sand & Gravel*, the annual publication of the Southern Appalachian Writers Cooperative. He lives in Cincinnati with his wife Elissa Pogue.

www.ingramcontent.com/pod-product-compliance
Lightning Source LLC
Chambersburg PA
CBHW070205100426
42743CB00013B/3063